LifeCaps Presents:

Joy:

The Unofficial Biography of miracle Mop Inventor, Joy Mangano

By Fergus Mason

BOOKCAPS

BookCaps™ Study Guides

www.bookcaps.com

Table of Contents

About LifeCaps

LifeCaps is an imprint of BookCaps™ Study Guides. With each book, a lesser-known or sometimes forgotten life is recapped. We publish a wide array of topics (from baseball and music to literature and philosophy), so check our growing catalogue regularly (www.bookcaps.com) to see our newest books.

Introduction

When we think of inventors, there are a couple of stereotypes we all tend to fall back on. The most iconic perhaps is a mad scientist type with screwdrivers and tape measures bristling from the pockets of his lab coat, and probably with his face blackened by the explosion of his latest failed prototype. More realistically, we might think of a tech-savvy entrepreneur like Steve Jobs or James Dyson – someone with the vision to come up with an idea, and the time and resources to spend on turning it into reality.

What we probably *don't* imagine is a single mom living on Long Island's North Shore, working a succession of jobs to support herself and her three kids. In those circumstances, who has enough time to spare that they can see the need for a new invention, come up with a design, get a prototype made and tested, then get it into production and start marketing it?

Joy Mangano did. In fact she didn't do it just once – she's done it over and over again. Mangano is one of the most prolific inventors in the world today and she has an almost uncanny ability for coming up with the right idea at the right time. Over and over again she's taken a familiar object and come up with a radically new twist, one that's grabbed the attention of millions of people and persuaded them to part with hard cash for the pleasure of owning one of her innovations. And unlike many inventors, she's always focused on things that make life easier, less stressful or more pleasant for ordinary people – inventions that anyone can benefit from.

Mangano doesn't fit the popular idea of an inventor at all. She's not a scientist or an engineer. She doesn't spend all her time in a shed full of power tools making ingenious but alarming gadgets. These days she's as likely to be on Home Shopping Network demonstrating one of her many products as she is to be testing a prototype, because for more than a decade she's been the undoubted star of the retail channel. Millions of people have seen her enthusiastic performances, and been convinced to try out her latest idea as a result. She's now the head of a multimillion-dollar business that she's created from nothing, just by applying her formidable ingenuity. So how did a lone parent from New York come to be such a powerhouse of innovation? What is Joy Mangano's secret?

Well, that's a good question. Mangano doesn't have a history of winning school science fairs or building gadgets at home. She just seems to have a talent for spotting good ideas, and then turning them into reality. From the moment as a teenager when she realized her plans were practical she's never hesitated to act when she believes she's come up with something worth doing. It turns out that, usually, all it takes is that initiative and a bit of determination – and Mangano has plenty of both. She's already developed more new products than just about anyone else and no doubt there are more to come. Let's look at her amazing history.

Chapter 1: Early Experiments

Joy Mangano was born in East Meadow, New York, in 1956. Italian-Americans, the Manganos were great believers in initiative and entrepreneurship; her father ran a business that hired out school buses and airport shuttles, and her mother helped out in the office. It was a family where energy and ambition were valued and Joy picked up on it from an early age. She also showed an insatiable curiosity for electrics and mechanics – anything to do with how things worked. "I was blowing up toasters in my parents' house when I was little," she recalled in an interview.[i]

It would have been understandable if Joy's parents had some doubts about their daughter's technical experiments but instead, they encouraged her – just as long as she didn't blow up the house. As she grew older she started spending some of her spare time at her father's business, watching his mechanics work on buses and building up an untrained but thorough understanding of how engineering works. She started to try things out for herself; if she saw a device that interested her she'd try to build a better one.

At the same time she was doing well at school, both academically and in sports. In fact, she did so well she graduated high school a year early. Somehow she'd managed to be an honors student and high school athlete while also taking part in other hobbies and working a string of part-time jobs. It wasn't high school that planted the seeds of her future success, though; it was an idea she had while working at one of those jobs.

Aged sixteen, Joy was working in a local animal shelter in Huntington. Huntington is a fairly prosperous place and many families have pets. As a volunteer at the shelter Joy looked after those that had strayed or needed adoption, feeding them and helping with basic health care. It wasn't long before she became depressingly familiar with one of the major hazards to suburban pets – traffic. Too many of the shelter's residents were dogs and cats who'd survived an encounter with a car, often with horrific injuries, and naturally Joy wondered how it might be possible to reduce this toll. It wasn't long before she had an idea.

Domestic pets, like any other animal, are tempting targets for a whole range of parasites and one of the main health concerns for a pet owner is keeping these away from their furry companion. Cats and dogs are particularly bothered by fleas, tiny, wingless insects that puncture an animal's skin with their sharp mouths and drink their blood. Fleas aren't usually a major health problem in themselves but they can carry – and transmit – a range of diseases. In fact, the infamous Black Death, the plague that devastated Europe in the 14th century and killed nearly half the population, was probably spread by infected fleas. That's less of a concern in suburban New York but fleas are still a nuisance; their itchy bites are very irritating to pets, and they're quite happy to bite the owners, too. Animal shelters usually treat their residents with shampoos or skin drops but for owners that isn't always convenient, as anyone who's tried to medicate a cat knows. Instead the most common option is a flea collar. This is just a normal pet collar but the lining is treated with an insecticide that's harmless to the pet but lethal to fleas; it gradually spreads through the animal's skin, poisoning any flea that bites it.

Because most pets that go outdoors wear flea collars, Joy realized this could be a way to make them more visible to drivers. The inner surface of the collar was an absorbent material that held the insecticide, but the outer surface could be pretty much anything. If it could be made from a reflective or fluorescent material it would mean animals could be seen in a car's headlights from much further away.

Joy was convinced she was onto a good idea here, but now she had no idea what to do with it. She was a teenager; she had no business knowledge, no idea how to go about securing a patent or having her design turned into prototypes that she could test. For a few weeks she pondered on her inspiration, thinking of ways she could improve it as well as any possible option for making it a reality. In the end, though, she just didn't know what to do next and she decided to leave it for now. After all she could come back to it later, when she knew how to turn it into a commercial product.

Unfortunately that's not the way it turned out. The year after Joy had her idea, pet products giant Hartz Mountain Corporation put a very similar collar on the market – a flea collar with a bright, reflective outer surface.

It's often implied that if Joy had known what to do with her idea she could have had it on the market first, and made a fortune from it. The reality probably isn't so simple. Hartz is a huge company, one of the largest suppliers of pet foods and accessories in North America and the UK. The chances are their collar had been in development for far longer than a year before it appeared in stores, and that as soon as they got wind of any plan by Joy to market a similar one they would simply have released it early. However, it did teach her a valuable lesson: an idea for a new product was no good unless you picked it up and ran with it, turning it into something that could be stacked on a shelf and sold.

It would be a while before Joy had time to come up with any more inventions, though. After high school she enrolled at Pace University, a private college with campuses in New York City and Westchester County, for a degree in business administration. She graduated in 1978 and then, at 22 years old, seems to have decided it was time to find a conventional career and start a family. She was already well on track towards that; she was dating fellow business student Tony Miranne,[ii] and they married soon after graduation. For a while Joy worked as reservations manager for an airline, but by her mid-20s she decided the time had come to think about children. In 1982 her first daughter was born and soon the couple added two more girls to their household.

Sometimes things don't work out, though, and by the late 1980s the marriage was in trouble. Joy and Tony still got on well enough but it was obvious they weren't really compatible as a couple. In 1989 they divorced and she found herself living in a small, two-bedroom ranch house in Smithtown, a community on Long Island's North Shore with a large Italian-American community. With herself and her three daughters the house was cramped, and there was also the constant struggle to pay bills and put food on the table. She took on extra work, waiting tables at the weekend to cover her expenses. It was a struggle, but unlike many single parents she could see a potential way out of it – her talent for invention.

Chapter 2: Paying the Bills

As a working single parent Joy Mangano didn't have a lot of spare time. After a day at work she would arrive home and launch right into another full schedule of looking after her kids and getting the housework done. Keeping an apartment clean and tidy is a not insignificant amount of work and every week she had to spend hours vacuuming, dusting, sweeping, etc. Of course, technology has made many of these tasks easier over the last few decades. A dishwasher saves a lot of time over washing dishes by hand. Vacuuming can be tedious, but it's much easier than using a carpet sweeper or broom – and it gets your carpets cleaner, too. Modern cleaning products make it possible to get hygienic, sparkling surfaces without hours of elbow grease with a damp cloth. Housework is hard and time-consuming, but less so than it used to be.

Then you get the mop out to clean the kitchen floor.

The familiar image of a mop is the sort of thing that appears in Tom and Jerry cartoons and every movie scene you've ever seen where the heroes walk past a bored cleaner – a wooden handle with a clump of wet, grubby yarn hanging off one end. Mops have been around for a long, long time; the first reference to a mop - spelled "mappe" at the time - is in an English document dated 1596 (despite the different spelling it's pronounced the same way; English vowels have changed through the centuries). The design has changed over time but the basic principle has always been the same – sweep the floor with a broom, then use a bunch of wet yarn or fabric to swab away stains, clean up any remaining dust and put a final polish on the surface. Mops are versatile though – they're also the quickest and easiest way to clear up spilled liquids. Until the 19th century they were often made at home. Families would thread rags onto a long nail – sometimes a special wide-headed mop nail bought from a local blacksmith – and hammer it into the end of a wooden handle. Later ready-made mop heads became widely available, and ever since then people have been trying to improve the design.

A mop is effective, but it's far from perfect. Its capacity to soak up liquid, whether it's spilled coffee or dirty water from washing the floor, is limited, and when that capacity is reached it stops picking up liquid and just moves it around. That means mopping is frequently interrupted while you squeeze as much fluid as possible out of the mop head and into a bucket. That can be a messy and inefficient process, and since at least 1837 inventors have been trying to find a way to improve it. For many decades the most common was a mop dryer, a metal (or later plastic) bowl perforated with dozens of holes, either built into the top of a specialized mop bucket or clipped onto a standard one. The mop head is pressed down into the dryer, forcing out most of the liquid it contains. It works reasonably well, but it's crude and can take a lot of force to get the mop dry enough. Most people who've done a lot of mopping have had the awful expedience of pressing just a bit too hard, at slightly the wrong angle, and feeling the bucket suddenly shift. A second later there's a clattering sound and a wave of frothy gray water sweeps across the almost-clean floor, undoing all your hard work and putting you right back at the beginning.

By the 1950s more sophisticated mop buckets were available, usually larger-sized professional ones that were often mounted on wheels. These had a perforated or slotted compartment the fabric or yarn of the mop head could be inserted into, and a lever that would squeeze the compartment walls tightly together. It's possible to squeeze a lot more water out using this method, and there's almost no risk of upsetting the bucket over your feet, but they never really caught on for home use. Instead there was a steady move toward flat mops. These replaced the traditional head with a strip of absorbent foam or cloth, attached to a flat head with a hinge in the middle. A lever or slide on the mop handle could be operated to press the two halves of the head tightly together, forcing liquid out of the absorbent pad. These devices had the big advantage that because the squeezing mechanism was built in to the mop itself they could be used with a normal bucket, and there was no risk at all of knocking it over.

Flat mops have their own problems, though. Because the flat pads have less volume than a traditional mop they absorb less liquid before needing squeezed. Some people prefer their ease of use; others would rather have something that allows more mopping before being wrung out. The result is that for years the market has been split between flat mops and the more traditional style, often with strips of microfiber cloth replacing the yarn. Either kind will get the floor mopped, but neither is perfect.

Like most people Joy got by as best she could with the products that were available, but she wasn't really satisfied with any of them. She had another issue with mops, too. In addition to having a home to keep clean she had also been a keen boater for years, and being around boats involves a surprising amount of mopping. Every yacht has a mop on board, often lashed to a rail on the cabin roof or clipped to the shrouds with its head streaming in the wind like a grubby, ironic pennant. Swabbing down the decks is part of the daily routine for any proud boat owner, but it's not an easy job. Nobody bothers with a bucket – it's easier to just dip the mop over the side – so there's no simple way to wring the wet head out, and flat mops never caught on; they're too bulky and prone to snagging on ropes, wires and fittings. Most boaters wring the dirty water over the side with their hands, which is effective but not all that pleasant. Then, not long after moving to Smithtown, she realized she could apply her creative talents to making the job easier – and just maybe come up with a best-selling product at the same time. All she had to do was invent a better mop.

There were two challenges that had to be overcome if Joy was to come up with a mop that beat everything else on the market. Flat mops were easy to use but didn't absorb much; traditional ones could soak up a lot more liquid but were trickier, and often messier, to work with. What she had to do was to combine the best aspects of both and create a design that would both hold large quantities of liquid and be easy to squeeze out. That meant some sort of built-in squeezing mechanism, but the standard flat design was obviously out; it wouldn't be difficult to simply make the pad thicker, but then the force needed to squeeze it effectively would mean the whole thing had to be very heavily (and expensively) constructed. Joy wanted something manageable and affordable, but still highly effective.

The first decision was what material to make the head from. There were several options. Most new mops used some form of synthetics; microfiber blends were popular, because they were cheap and reasonably absorbent. They could be manufactured as layered pads, fabric strips or even, at a slightly higher cost, as yarn-like strands. Alternatively sponge pads or strips could be used. Sponge strips were fragile though, and it turned out there was a problem with flat mops in general; if sand, grit or even small pieces of broken glass got caught in the pad it could result in a badly scratched floor. The squeezing mechanisms also made the handles bulky, so it was more difficult to mop out tight corners or restricted spaces. That could be a major drawback when it came to cleaning around commodes or behind appliances. It seemed important to come up with a design that kept the handle as slip as possible, while also building in a squeezing mechanism.

Then Joy had an idea. If you don't have a mop dryer the best way to squeeze out a traditional mop is to grab the ends of the yarn strands and twist them. She realized there was a way to make a mechanism to twist the strands *without* getting your hands wet – and she immediately started designing a mop that would do it.

The heart of the new design was in its absorbent material. Joy opted for cotton, as it's a highly absorbent natural material, and as long as it's kept clean it doesn't scratch any surface. Instead of a bundle of short strands, though, she started with a continuous loop made up of 300 feet of cotton yarn. This was threaded repeatedly through not one but two heads and these, in turn, were fixed to the inner and outer tubes of a telescopic handle. With the inner tube pulled fully in the heads were nested close together and the yarn hung loosely in a bundle of loops, which worked just like the strands of a traditional mop – absorbing liquid and buffing the floor. Push the inner handle out, though, and the mop head immediately changed shape; now the two heads were about a foot and a half apart with the cotton stretched between, running endlessly back and forth between the two perforated plastic disks. Then, all you had to do to wring out the mop head was twist the outer handle; the disk attached to it rotated, while the other one stayed still, and the cotton was twisted tightly around the inner tube – quickly and effectively squeezing out almost all the liquid it held. It had the liquid capacity of a traditional mop but was as easy to squeeze out as a flat one – and it didn't need a mop dryer.

Joy now had an idea for her perfect mop, but she needed more than an idea; she needed a product, and she didn't have the equipment to make it herself. The solution was to find an engineer who was intrigued by her design, who helped her produce a prototype. That then had to be tested and tweaked, because no new design ever works perfectly the first time. Finally, everything seemed to work the way she wanted. Now, if she was going to market her invention, she needed some stock. Producing and perfecting the prototype had eaten most of her savings so she borrowed money from friends and family, then found a factory that was willing to produce a small batch – she ordered 100 mops. That was all she could afford; by the time she'd paid for them, on top of what she'd spent on having engineering drawings made, the prototype produced and a patent submitted to prevent anyone stealing her design, the project had cost her close to $100,000.[iii]

Capitalization is one of the biggest obstacles to bringing a new invention to market – probably the biggest – and Joy was lucky she'd managed to overcome it. Now a load of long cardboard packing cases arrived at her home; they contained the first batch of her new product. In the space of less than a year she had gone from an idea to a stack of finished mops. But that wasn't the end of the story. She had the stock, but if she couldn't sell it the money she'd sunk into her ambition would be gone and she would have a very difficult time paying it back. This is another challenge for the lone inventor; a major company can develop a product then market it through their advertising budget and retail channels. Joy was on her own. She had to find potential customers and persuade them to buy her mops, and none of her work experience covered marketing. That put her at a serious disadvantage; after all, there was no shortage of competitors in the mop market, including some long-established direct sales companies and major home products manufacturers like O-

Cedar and Rubbermaid. Joy was convinced that her mop was better than theirs, but they had a huge head start when it came to putting products in front of customers.

Joy knew her limitations when it came to marketing, and realized that it would be hard to break in to a flooded market. She hadn't made it this far by doing things the conventional way though; she decided there must be other ways to find customers. Her first idea was to sell it to boat owners, so she spent more money putting adverts in yachting magazines. Then she started giving demonstrations at boat shows along the North Shore, explaining how what she'd christened the Marine Mop would swab a deck without scratching and could be easily wrung out over the side with a simple twist of the handle. Some sales trickled in – it was a good product, easy to use and effective, and it had another big advantage on board a boat; it floated. Accidentally drop it over the side and it would hang around for you to go back and pick it up, unlike some flat mops with metal levers.

Unfortunately it soon became obvious that there just weren't enough yachts to turn a profit selling mops to their owners. There was no reason to restrict herself to that market though; the Marine Mop worked just as well in a bathroom as on a boat, and in the unlikely event she'd had any doubts about that the people who were buying them at boat shows would have put her straight; "I'm going to use this in my kitchen," some of them said. Joy thought, "Fine. So I'm going to sell them to everyone who has a kitchen."

She was confident that anyone who saw the product would recognize its potential, so she decided to keep on demonstrating it in person; that meant spending a lot of her spare time going round Long Island stores showing off her invention, which had now been hastily rebranded as the Miracle Mop to make it appeal to a more general audience. Some stores were happy with the mops they already had in stock; others decided the Miracle Mop was interesting enough that they would take a few and see how they sold. And, perhaps to their surprise, they did sell.

Thanks to Joy's efforts the first batch of a hundred mops was sold in a few weeks. The money they brought in, and the last of the money she'd borrowed, paid for another batch – then another, larger one. After a year, working out of an improvised office in her bedroom, she had done far better than most inventors ever do – she'd ordered, and sold, several increasingly large consignments of mops; several thousand people had been persuaded to give her design a try. With no real marketing budget behind her, and no established retail channels, it was an amazing achievement. But it wasn't enough.

The sales she'd achieved had brought in about $10,000 but that was nowhere near enough for her to live on, never mind starting to repay the money she'd borrowed. The Miracle Mop had made an impact on the market but it wasn't a viable business proposition. Some of Joy's friends started trying to persuade her to give up on it and carry on with her normal career; it had been a brave attempt but, they said, it was crazy to carry on trying to sell such a mundane product. "A mop is a mop is a mop," she remembers them saying. But Joy didn't agree. Potential customers tended to share her friends' feelings at first but, once she demonstrated her product, their opinion changed quickly – "I have to have that." She was convinced that if she could show the Miracle Mop to enough people the sales would come in.

The first thing she had to do, if she was going to make a career out of selling her ideas, was get herself set up as a proper business. So far she was working out of an improvised office in the corner of her bedroom; with herself and three young girls – her oldest wasn't ten years old yet – crammed into a two-bedroom house there simply wasn't enough room to have a dedicated room for work. And the amount of work was growing. She had to manage invoices, get new stock ordered and deal with her earnings as well as trying to pick a workable product from the ideas that constantly fizzed in her mind. She urgently needed a proper office.

Her father, seeing how well the Miracle Mop was selling, stepped forward with a solution. His bus and shuttle business had a body shop in Deer Park, and there was an unused office there. Joy could use it, he decided. That was a huge step forward; now she had enough space to work in comfortably, keep samples and even hold some stock. She quit the jobs she'd been working to support herself and incorporated a new company, Arma Products. This was the moment to roll the dice; she had just gambled it all on being able to break in to the mainstream market. But how?

Chapter 3: Finding an Audience

Home retail channels are now a mainstay of cable TV and can be found all over the world, but they're very much an American invention and they have an interesting history. The whole vast industry came into existence because of a bizarre and unlikely business hiccup at a small Florida radio station.

In 1977 Bob Circosta, an aspiring media personality, was hosting a news talk show on Clearwater-based WWQT. His ambition was to break into national broadcasting as a news anchor and he was working hard at local radio as a stepping stone to that, but in the meantime he had to deal with the realities of a small station, and one of those was advertising. Without the revenue from broadcasting commercials small stations can't survive, but many of the local businesses who fill the slots have cash flow difficulties of their own. In July 1977 one of WWQT's advertisers, a hardware store, contacted the station to say they couldn't pay their advertising bill and offered to pay in goods instead. In lieu of cash they suggested giving the station a consignment of that archetypal mid-70s kitchen appliance, the Rival electric can opener, in a fetching shade of olive green. The station wasn't exactly overwhelmed at this offer but, deciding to make the best of a bad job, they accepted. Perhaps, they thought, they'd be able to sell the can openers on the air.

Of course that meant nominating a salesman, and much to his disgust Bob Circosta found himself nominated.[iv]

Circosta decided to make the best of it though, mostly as a favor to station owner Lowell "Bud" Paxson, and one sunny July afternoon he finished his talk segment and then began talking about can openers. In fact he didn't just *talk* about can openers; he *raved* about them, pouring on the enthusiasm as he extolled their convenience, efficiency and of course the great price – only $9.95 apiece. And, to his amazement, it worked; a few minutes into his spiel calls started coming in from listeners with their credit card in their hands and an empty can opener-sized space in their kitchens. All 112 sold in less than an hour.

Paxson had had his doubts about taking the can openers, but Circosta's success made him think. If it could be repeated there was the prospect of a tempting new revenue stream for the station, and like most small businessmen Paxson wasn't going to let one of those slip through his fingers. A few weeks after the can opener sale he tried again, with the same format and a different product; again, Circosta came through and sales were strong. Before long it became a daily five-minute segment, Suncoast Bargaineers. Every day at 2pm Circosta would introduce a new product, extol its virtues and offer it to WWQT listeners at a bargain price – and, every day, orders would come in.

It didn't take long before Paxson realized the sales model had the potential to make more money than the station itself did, so he leased a Tampa cable TV channel and started running a three-hour sales slot every day. The new service, Home Shopping Channel, was a friendly, almost amateurish affair; at the end of every hour the sales team would ask viewers if they should stay on for another hour and if enough called in to request that they'd do it. It was popular though – so popular that in 1985 the company rebranded itself as Home Shopping Network and went nationwide. It also became a 24-hour service, so aspirational housewives – the typical viewer was a female homemaker in their 40s – could shop around the clock.

The runaway success of HSN soon sparked imitators, and the most successful was QVC. Founded less than a year after HSN went national, the new network, whose initials stand for Quality, Value, Convenience, got an early boost when Sears signed up for a two-year deal. Originally QVC was on the air evenings during the week and all day at weekends but before long it was doing well enough to go to constant broadcasting and start buying up smaller competitors. There were ups and downs, but through the late 1980s and into the early 90s it built up a strong following among TV shoppers. Then in early 1992 Joy Mangano approached them with an offer. She had a consignment of mops; would they like to try selling them?

QVC weren't sure; their product range tended more towards zirconium jewelry and kitchen accessories. Joy was persuasive though, and QVC reluctantly agreed to take a thousand Miracle Mops. Soon they were being demonstrated daily on the channel – but sales were disappointing. After a few weeks, with most of the mops still in stock, QVC contacted Joy and asked her to take them back. They were grateful for the opportunity, they said, but they "really didn't sell mops".

Joy suspected that the fact QVC didn't really sell mops was the problem; it wasn't a product they were familiar with and that was coming across on air. Viewers weren't likely to hand over cash for a product that the presenters didn't understand and weren't very interested in. So Joy made QVC a counter-offer: Let her demonstrate the mops herself to a live audience and see how that turned out. If they still didn't sell she would take them back.

So now her belief in the product would be put to the test. She was confident that if she could show it to potential buyers they'd be as enthusiastic as she was, and her experiences around local stores and trade shows had reinforced that. Now she had the chance to demonstrate it in person to an audience of millions. It was a make or break moment that would decide the future of both the Miracle Mop and Joy's future as an entrepreneur. If this didn't work out she'd have few choices left, and would probably have to go back to her career and start repaying the money she'd borrowed. It's hard to spot doubts behind her overwhelming confidence, but she must have been feeling some stress as she stood on the QVC set that day with a mop in her hands watching the countdown tick towards zero. Then, on the wall behind the klieg lights and crews, a green bulb blinked out and a red one came on. The cameras were live and it was all up to her.

Twenty minutes later the cameras spun down and the green light came on. Hot, exhausted and apprehensive, Joy turned to the producer as he hurried out from behind the cameras. She'd given it her best shot and now she would find out how well she'd done. How many of the mops had she managed to shift?

The answer was staggering. In an hour her energy and enthusiasm had sold all the remaining stock, and then some. In fact more than 18,000 people had called in to buy a Miracle Mop. QVC wouldn't be sending any of them back to Joy; now they were asking her for extra stock to honor the sales they'd made. It was the breakthrough she'd been looking for. With ongoing sales through QVC she would be able to continue marketing the Miracle Mop and pay off the loans.

From then on Joy became a regular on QVC. Her unbounded enthusiasm and almost hyperactive demonstrations ensured continued sales, and a decade later Miracle Mop sales were averaging $10 million every year. Perhaps QVC hadn't really sold mops before, but they certainly did now. Joy had made it as an inventor, with her product in millions of homes across the USA; she'd achieved the success that eludes all but a handful of new ideas, and turned her design into a career.

But it wasn't enough. She had more ideas, more products she thought people might want to buy, and before the excitement surrounding the Miracle Mop's success had begun to fade she was already thinking about what she should do next.

Chapter 4: Industrial Empires

The first thing to do was to build herself up as a proper business. She had incorporated Arma Products to market the Miracle Mop, but it was still more or less a one-woman show. Sometimes her children helped her fill orders, packing the mops for her and learning how to fill out shipping forms. It was working, but if she wanted to expand – and she did – it wasn't going to keep working for long. It's not too hard to operate on your own if you're providing a service – accountancy, for example, or graphic design – but if you need to ship goods to a large number of customers you'll quickly be overwhelmed; just arranging shipping will soon take all your time, leaving none for marketing, doing the books or developing products. Joy's sales had gone from a few dozen mops a week to thousands every day; she needed to handle ordering new stock, getting supplies to distributors and filling the orders that were still coming in from boaters, as well as appearing on QVC. It was time to build a more professional organization.

Joy's father was happy for her to work out of his body shop, but there were limits to how much she could expand – he needed the premises, too. There was no problem with her using the old offices but she couldn't take over space in the actual workshop. A move was going to be necessary. Luckily, with the success of her QVC debut, she had the funds to find a location of her own. After some searching she settled on Edgewood, New York. A small hamlet in the town of Hunter, located less than a mile and a half from her existing location in Deer Park[v], Edgewood was home to a business estate with vacant, affordable industrial units. Leasing one of them would give her both her own offices, room for more staff and the vital warehouse space she'd need to handle large quantities of stock.

Joy was still operating as Arma Products but
now she decided it was time to find a new name
that gave a better idea of what the company was
all about. The solution was simple, but perfect; in
late 1992, not long after her first QVC
appearance, she changed the name of the
business to Ingenious Designs, Inc. It's hard to
think of a name that encapsulates Joy's mission
more neatly than that one.

It was QVC that helped Joy to make her breakthrough, and the Miracle Mop continued to sell well as she worked on setting up her new premises, but the network's rivals were always on the lookout for new products of their own and it wasn't long before Joy came to their attention. In addition to the Miracle Mop she was now promoting a range of other products, too, including new designs of cake boxes and other kitchen items – some of them her own designs, others in association with their manufacturers. Through the 1990s the whole industry watched Ingenious Designs – and Joy's reputation – grow. It was clear that she had a genius for both coming up with her own products and identifying others that, while not well known, had a lot of potential. Her premises in Edgewood steadily expanded, until they were employing over 200 people and covered 100,000 square feet of factory, office and warehouse space.

By 1995 sales of the Miracle Mop alone exceeded $1 million annually, which is pretty good for a $14.95 item. Its popularity had expanded beyond QVC too – Kmart was selling thousands of them, and it had become a popular item at Home Depot as well. There were even special editions. Upscale department store chain Bloomingdale's decided they would like to stock them, and to add a touch of glamour they asked Joy to give them something out of the ordinary. She obliged, with a version molded from gold-colored plastic. It was just as efficient and affordable as the standard Miracle Mop but had a classy appearance that suited the chain's image. It also acted as an icebreaker, making a product that had achieved fame on shopping channels acceptable to Bloomingdale's status-conscious customers. The special edition was only available for a year, but standard Miracle Mops are still a favorite item in the store's product range.

With the Miracle Mop's growing popularity in mainstream retailers it was becoming obvious that Joy's personal fortunes weren't inextricably bound to her appearances on QVC. By the late 1990s Home Shopping Network were increasingly interested in building a relationship with her, and in 1999 they made their move.

HSN had come a long way in 22 years. The days of Bob Circosta and his box of can openers were far behind them; in 1986 it had expanded beyond cable, setting up a subsidiary – Silver King Broadcasting – that bought several terrestrial TV channels and added HSN retail shows to their programming. It was possible to tune in to HSN on virtually any TV in the United States, and the weekly audience ran to tens of millions. Sister channels were set up in Germany, Japan, Canada, Italy, the Philippines and the UK (although the British one went out of business in 2005). In 1999 HSN expanded even further, with the launch of HSN.com. That placed them firmly in the online retail market, which was a fraction of the size it is now but was already shaping up to be a huge future sales channel.

There were also changes at the top. HSN had become a billion dollar business, and had grown far beyond what Bud Paxson had ever expected it to. It was also becoming far too much work; Paxson was now in his sixties and wanted to retire. Luckily for him, at that point Barry Diller came along.

Barry Diller was a UCLA dropout who had been born into a San Francisco Jewish family in 1942. After he quit college his parents managed to find him a job in the mailroom at the William Morris Agency, but it was Diller himself who ended up being talent-spotted. In 1964 he was hired by ABC and a year later had worked his way up to Vice President of Development. His greatest achievement there was launching the ABC Movie of the Week, and ordering the first made-for-TV movies. In 1974 he moved to Paramount, where he became CEO at the age of just 32; after a decade he moved on to Fox, Inc. and worked there for another eight years. Then, in 1992, he became interested in shopping channels.

Leaving Fox, Diller paid $25 million for a share in QVC. He also tried to buy Paramount Corporation, but was outbid by Viacom. Not letting that put him off he spent three years at QVC, just as Joy was making her mark there with the Miracle Mop. Perhaps he kept her in mind when he left the network in 1995. Two years after that he approached Bud Paxson and made an offer for both Silver King Broadcasting, HSN's network of TV channels, and for HSN itself. Paxson accepted the offer and retired, while Diller set about a major reorganization of HSN. After his time at QVC he was skeptical about having so many channels solely dedicated to shopping, and started spinning off Silver King's stations into semi-independent ones with their own programming. He also purchased the USA Network, another cable and satellite TV business, and merged all the channels into USA Broadcasting, Inc. with the exception of HSN's dedicated retail channels. That left a more focused, professional shopping business, but now he wanted a superstar to draw in more viewers and sales. He chose Joy Mangano. Joy's own business was continuing to grow and thrive. In 1997 London-based professional services specialist Ernst & Young recognized her as one of the US recipients of their Entrepreneur of the Year award;[vi] other American winners that year included Mark Hughes of Herbalife, Jerry Yang and Tim Koogle of Yahoo and Jeff Bezos of Amazon.com. That award helped cement her position as one of the USA's most innovative businesspeople, and that plus her record at QVC made her a natural candidate for Diller. In late 1999 he approached her and offered to buy her company.

That must have been a tough decision. Joy had built Ingenious Designs herself from the ground up – she'd brought it all the way from a desk in the corner of her bedroom to a major operation with a multimillion-dollar annual turnover. Selling it to a huge corporation would be a blow; she wouldn't be fully in control any longer. Many entrepreneurs are inspired by the feeling of freedom, of being their own boss, and it can be very hard to give it up.

On the other hand, there were definite benefits in accepting the offer. First, it would give her a lot more financial backing. Even for a successful business, Long Island is an expensive place to work. It's even worse when the business needs to have large premises, like Ingenious Design did. Then there was the matter of time. Joy still found herself spending too much of her time handling day to day administration, and that reduced her ability to come up with new products. She needed more time to work on her designs, and being part of a larger corporation would take a lot of the routine matters off her shoulders. The backing of HSN would also make it easier to access draftsmen, engineers and prototyping services, which would be a huge help. Diller obviously had faith in her and her gifts, so she knew she would be able to count on their full support. Finally, as the icing on the cake, Diller was offering her a major role on HSN. She'd been able to build a substantial business by appearing on QVC; HSN, with more airtime and more viewers, opened up a whole new range of possibilities.

Diller's proposal needed careful thought, but in the end there was only one possible decision; Joy accepted the offer and Ingenious Designs became part of the HSN group. How she had the resources and the time to develop a new product, one that would establish her reputation on HSN the way the Miracle Mop had done for her on QVC. And she thought she knew just what it might be.

Chapter 5: The Best Selling product

Coat hangers are a pretty simple item, and you wouldn't think there was a lot that could be done to improve them. That's not to say they're perfect, of course. There are two main types: the bulky, curved sort made of molded plastic or – much more rarely, now – wood, which tend to hold your clothes more securely and don't create wrinkles at the shoulders, but take up a lot of closet space. Then there is the cheap wire type which is a lot more compact but has a whole list of other issues. They're easily bent, clothes often slip from them to end up as a crumpled heap on the floor of your closet, and their thin profile can create unsightly creases in very obvious places. These flaws are things most of us have just gotten used to living with, but that wasn't good enough for Joy Mangano.

The problems with coat hangers aren't complicated; they're just annoying. The more Joy looked at them the more she was convinced she could come up with a simple but effective design that would sort out all the existing issues and create either the perfect hanger or something pretty close to it.

First, she had to decide on the shape. A priority was that they minimized the closet space needed to hang each garment. That meant using a flat shape, which was also good for storage – flat hangers could be stacked neatly when they weren't being used. With that decision made she needed to find the right material. Steel was tempting, but ultimately unsuitable; the only way to make a light steel hanger is to make it from wire, and that brings too many problems with it. One of the biggest is that unless the wire is made from expensive, high grade steel the result will be flimsy and prone to bending. That's useful when you need a bit of wire to fish your key ring out of a drain, but not so good for hanging heavy winter coats. So steel was out. The standard plastic used for hangers was no good either; like wood, to get the required strength it had to be too bulky.

The solution finally turned out to be plastic, but not the slightly brittle stuff usually used for hangers. Joy found a hard nylon blend that was just flexible enough to avoid splitting, but tough enough that it wouldn't deform or snap even with a heavy garment on it. In fact, when molded into flat hangers a quarter inch thick, it turned out to be practically unbreakable in normal use. The new design had a rectangular cross-section with rounded corners and was just thick enough that it wouldn't put unwanted creases in whatever was hanging from it, and it was also light – almost as light as a wire hanger, and a lot tougher. It was also much stronger than traditional plastic hangers and less than half as thick.

Joy came up with two basic styles for her new hanger: an open-bottomed one for shirts and coats, and one with a bottom bar for hanging pants and suits. Thanks to the material she'd chosen the open design was strong enough to hold a heavy coat without flexing, but the shape she chose minimized weight and reduced the chance of causing wrinkles even more. Then she started thinking about new ways to use hangers more efficiently. Clips that snap over the bottom bar of a hanger are already familiar; they let skirts be hung up without folding them over the bar, which can crease them. An improved design of those was an obvious addition. Then she came up with something completely new. She called it the Cascading Hook, and it was a simple as it was ingenious. A light but strong plastic hook that could be slipped over the steel hook of a shirt hanger, or clipped to the bottom bar of a suit one, it allowed a second hanger to be hooked on to it. A ladder-like cascade of storage space could be created, but only using as much of the closet bar as a single hanger would. It was the perfect solution for lighter garments like shirts or blouses and while most of the improvements Joy had made so far were evolutionary, this one was revolutionary. No other brand of hangers had anything like it. Yet again she'd looked at a problem and come up with a solution so obvious everyone else had managed to miss it.

But there was one problem left, and it was a fundamental issue with the nylon material. It had a smooth surface, and it was slippery. Shirts or coats hung on it slid off even more easily than they did from a wire hanger. That was a potentially fatal flaw in the design – who wanted a hanger that deposited everything in a heap at the bottom of the closet? The hangers had to be given a non-slip surface, and there were a few ways to do that. The simplest was to mold them with a rough textured finish; that would work reasonably well, but it would be unattractive, and Joy, who likes designs that are elegant as well as practical, wasn't happy with the idea. Then she had a better idea, one adapted from car manufacturers.

Large parts of a car's interior appear to be coated in a slightly fuzzy fabric, but they aren't really. Instead they're molded plastic panels that have been coated with flocking. Flocking is a simple but effective process. The panels are first treated with a layer of adhesive, and then tiny lengths of fine fiber are stuck to it. This is usually done by giving the fibers a negative electrical charge, then earthing the panel and releasing the fibers near it. The charge they carry is attracted to the earthed panel and the result is they hit it end-on and are caught by the adhesive. It gives a texture that's soft to the touch, has a high-quality appearance and (if the right glue is used) is very durable. More importantly, it's also non-slip.

Car interior flocking doesn't usually get much in the way of wear and tear – the parts that suffer from that are usually covered with leather or fabric – so it was vital to do some trials and find an adhesive that would stand up to having clothes slipped on and off frequently. There's no shortage of adhesives available though, and before long one was found that resulted in a robust, velvety finish applied over the nylon of the hangers. That solved the biggest remaining problem and the result was an attractive product that Joy knew was going to be a success. All that remained was to find a name that would be as evocative as the now-famous Miracle Mop.

Getting the name right was vital. As good as the new design was, it wasn't the sort of thing people were going to notice unless it was really attention-grabbing; after all it was just a coat hanger. As Joy knew from the Miracle Mop, though, a name that stuck in people's minds would go a long way towards raising its profile. So, inspired by the product's plush feel, she dubbed them Huggable Hangers.

Huggable Hangers made their debut on Home Shopping Network in 2000, and this time Joy was there to demonstrate them right from the start; HSN had learned from Miracle Mops. It was a wise decision. The full quality of the hangers wasn't really obvious unless you could handle them for yourself but Joy's enthusiasm made it obvious that these weren't just any ordinary coat hanger. Within minutes orders started pouring in – and they kept on coming; fifteen years later they're still selling as well as ever. The Huggable Hanger is now HSN's best-selling product *ever*, with 300 million sold in the first ten years alone.

Obviously success brings its own challenges, and as the saying goes, imitation is the sincerest form of flattery. It wasn't long before unlicensed copies started to appear and today they're widespread. None of them come close to either the quality or the popularity of the original, though. Today the Huggable Hanger is still a regular on HSN and it's also available through conventional retail channels, too. Target stock them and they can be found easily on Amazon and many other online stores. For such a simple idea, based around such an unexciting product, it's become a huge success and a great testament to Joy's ingenuity and imagination.

Chapter 6: Forever Fragrant

Most of us have at least one air freshener at home. Whether it's an aerosol can that can be sprayed around, or a plastic case with a block of wobbly scented gel inside, they're a standard feature of modern life. Our ancestors, living in a world with primitive sewers and crude waste disposal methods, had little choice but to tolerate the occasional bad smell. In the sanitized world of the 21st century we have that choice, and we exercise it. It's not enough that our homes don't smell like septic tanks or rotting garbage; we want them to smell pleasant at all times. That's why any good-sized grocery store will have a shelf of products guaranteed to waft lavender, citrus or pine scents through your home.

The problem with most of these products, though, is that they look a bit industrial. They work well enough but, with a few exceptions, they're the sort of thing people try to hide away as much as possible. Is there any real reason for things to be that way though? Joy Mangano thought not. An air freshener isn't complicated, after all; it's just a container that holds something scented. Containers don't have to be purely functional – they can be made more attractive very easily. There's no law that says their scented contents have to be a lump of something green and wobbly either – that's just the cheapest way to do it.

Joy quickly decided that instead of waiting to come up with another radical product she might as well do something with the humble air freshener. It seemed like the ideal product for a home shopping channel, too; simple and affordable, the sort of thing that many people would buy on impulse if it looked good and was enthusiastically demonstrated. It also had the benefit of being easy to sell in multiples. That's an important advantage for retail channels like HSN. Once viewers decide to buy a product, many of them can easily be persuaded to upsize to a multipack. After all, if you're buying an air freshener for the bathroom, why not get a few and put one in every room – especially if there's a discount?

The approach she decided on was a simple one. Most air fresheners use purpose-designed containers that are efficient but not very attractive. Ironically, this means they're more expensive than they need to be, as well as uglier. There are other ways to make an air freshener than a block of gel in a perforated plastic box, though. The gel is just a substrate – a substance that holds the actual freshener, and releases it gradually. The freshener itself is a mixture of chemicals that handle odors in various ways. Some are absorbent – activated charcoal or silica gel will trap the airborne particles that cause unpleasant smells. Others, like chlorine, hydrogen peroxide and ozone, chemically neutralize the particles. Finally, most fresheners contain a fragrance that will both mask nasty smells and give the air a new, more pleasant one. Gel is a cheap and convenient way to package these ingredients but it's far from the only one – they can be loaded into just about anything that's absorbent.

Air fresheners that use wicks or wooden reeds already existed and Joy decided to follow that model. Combined with some attractive, but inexpensive, off the shelf containers these reeds formed the basis of her new Forever Fragrant range. Some fresheners like this use plain reeds; liquid air freshener is poured into a container and the reeds are placed in it. The liquid is soaked up by the reeds and slowly evaporates into the air. These devices work well but they do have their disadvantages. The biggest one is that the container can be knocked over, spilling the liquid – which can damage some surfaces. The reeds, being soaked with liquid, also tend to attract dust; after a while they become less effective at dispersing the freshener. Instead, Joy decided to use pre-soaked reeds, sold in packs of twenty. Once the liquid they contained had evaporated they could simply be thrown away and replaced. She picked out a range of fragrances, and chose a design of jar to match each one. Then, as a bonus, she developed a complementary product in the same fragrances – scented candles. HSN fans could now buy an inexpensive set of three or four glass vases, a large supply of scented sticks and a matching candle in a decorative holder. Each item wasn't just effective – it was attractive, too.

Conventional air fresheners do have some advantages, though; they're more effective against very strong odors, for example, if you have lots of pets. For viewers who needed some extra deodorizing power, Joy came up with a slightly different solution. The Forever Fragrant AirFLO is a powered freshener, an elegant molded plastic vase shape that's available in a range of colors. It's obvious that Joy's talent was at work – while it's plastic its shape means it doesn't look out of place in even the most attractive room. It's also an extremely elegant piece of engineering, another Mangano trademark. Instead of relying on an aerosol can, like many powered fresheners do, it uses scented disks that simply slot into its body and release their fragrance as the device's fan draws air through their perforations. As an extra touch the disks can also be used on their own: placed in a drawer, linen cupboard or just in a discreet spot in any room they'll slowly fill the air with their scent – for up to two years.

An air freshener is a simple item, and it's not hard to make one that works, but what Joy did was to look beyond functionality and come up with something that looks good, too. The Forever Fragrant range is now a firm favorite on HSN, with millions of sets sold.

Chapter 7: Selling the Sizzle

Joy Mangano is best known as an inventor, but it's easy to argue that her true gift is as a saleswoman. Since early in her career in TV shopping she's shown a talent for finding useful products that aren't getting a lot of publicity, and using her distinctive style to market them. Sometimes the public gets confused, and thinks she actually invented them herself. Sometimes she did, other times she didn't, although she may come up with variations of the original product. One example of this is the Roly Kit, still a popular item on QVC. The Roly Kit is a toolbox with a difference. It's made up of a number of molded plastic compartments fixed to two strips of heavy nylon webbing. These roll up into a compact unit that snaps closed and can be carried securely, with no risk of anything falling out of the correct compartment. Unrolled, every compartment is easily accessible. None of the compartments are very large, so it never caught on in the construction industry, but it became quite popular among fishermen (it's an almost perfect tackle box) and jewelry makers (beads can easily jump between compartments when a normal toolbox gets bumped; that doesn't happen in a Roly Kit).

Joy started promoting the Roly Kit on QVC not long after her first appearances with the Miracle Mop, first selling the standard model and then a range of spin-offs that included small versions designed as jewelry boxes, and brightly colored ones aimed at children; they make good toy boxes, too. It's easy to understand why many people thought she had invented it, but she didn't – and in fact never claimed to have. In fact, the Roly Kit was designed in the Netherlands and has been on the market since 1979, when Joy had barely graduated college; the company set up to produce it, RolyKit Storage4All BV, is still in existence.

Actually, RolyKit BV proved to be a very useful contact for Joy. Like many European and American companies it outsources most of its actual manufacturing to China, and in RolyKit's case they have their own fabrication plant there. That gives them the best of both worlds; located in the west, they have access to the best design and marketing talent, but they can also take advantage of China's lower labor costs and highly-developed shipping networks.

RolyKit don't have a retail channel; at first they sold their products to retailers, but through the 1980s they increasingly started to act as an outsourced designer and manufacturer for other companies. Many of these clients wanted products – usually plastic storage solutions – to sell alongside their existing product lines, for example cosmetics giant Avon. The famous Avon ladies need to carry a lot of products for demonstration purposes, and normal makeup boxes are nowhere near big enough. Avon hired RolyKit to design and manufacture a special large case; it won a design award for the company.[vii] Other organizations they've produced unique goods for include WH Smith, L'Oreal, Agfa – and HSN.

While Joy was promoting the Roly Kit she realized that there were major advantages in having access to a company with its own production facilities, especially as she was looking at releasing another plastic product in the near future – the Huggable Hangers. Negotiations with RolyKit BV soon paid off and they agreed to manufacture the hangers for her. They also sent her more of their own designs, including pencil cases and cosmetics boxes based n the Roly Kit design. The partnership was extremely useful for both sides: RolyKit got a popular and persuasive representative on US shopping channels, and Joy had found a high quality manufacturer as well as a steady stream of products she could promote while her own new design was being perfected.

Sometimes Joy just takes an unexciting product and makes it fun. Many people who don't normally wear glasses do find they need a pair for reading, especially as they get older. Reading glasses just provide some clarity; they don't need to be carefully matched to your eyesight like prescription lenses do, so they're cheap and widely available. Most grocery stores stock a selection, as do pharmacies, bookshops and even some gas stations. Over the last few years they've become a fairly ubiquitous product – but they're also a pretty dull one. Usually they come in a couple of colors – black and brown are the most common – and don't have a lot in the way of styling. Like a Bic lighter or disposable pen they're simple, utilitarian products that get the job done but aren't something most people are going to get very excited about. In short, they were just waiting for the Joy Mangano touch.

Some research was enough to show Joy that basic reading glasses could be made a lot more colorful and fun without raising the price much – they could still be sold for a couple of dollars a pair. Alternatively they could be sold in sets, each pair a different color; that would let people match their reading glasses to their outfit, choose their favorite color and keep a couple of pairs for emergencies, or stash a pair everywhere they might need them rather than carrying them around all the time – one pair in the office, perhaps, another in the car and a third beside their favorite armchair at home. The aim was to give people more choice so she developed a range of sets, starting from three pairs of glasses – each with its own color-coded protective pouch – to high-end packages with seven or eight pairs and a set of bifocal sunglasses, often with a hard-shell case, stand or other accessories. Anyone who used reading glasses could find a set that met their needs, and they turned into yet another HSN hit; within a year of them going on the market more than a million pairs had been sold.

Becoming a high-profile businesswoman didn't just make Joy famous; it also gave her ideas for more products. Anyone who does a lot of traveling knows how difficult it can be to keep your clothes looking good, and hotel irons often leave a lot to be desired. When you suddenly find yourself in demand at trade shows, or having to visit factories to negotiate with the people who'll be making your products, the last thing you have time for is removing wrinkles from your clothes.

But there's a quick way to do it. If clothes have already been ironed, and just have a few minor creases they've picked up from being packed in a case or bag, steam will remove them. Lots of veteran travelers hang their shirts in the bathroom while they're showering, because the hot, humid air will help remove wrinkles. Laundry steamers use the same principle to take creases out of clothes that are too delicate to be ironed, or large items like bedding and curtains. Joy decided to put the same capability in a small, portable device that people could take with them when they traveled, and the result was My Little Steamer. About the size of a travel kettle, it runs on plain tap water and produces a jet of steam that removes wrinkles easily. It doesn't need an ironing board, and in fact, you don't even need to take the clothes off the hanger.

The steamer wasn't the only innovation for travelers Joy came up with. In cooperation with RolyKit she helped develop a new range of wheeled luggage, the Clothes It All system. This was based on traditional wheeled bags and cases but included convenient features like pockets for flight tickets, cosmetics organizers and laptop compartments.

Even fabrics haven't escaped Joy's magic touch. She's designed her own lines of bedding, which again aim for convenience and versatility – reversible duvet covers, and sheets with integrated bed skirts for easier washing and use. Her True Perfection towels use blended cotton and bamboo fabric and are far more stain-resistant than normal towels. It would be stretching a point to call any of these things inventions, but what's certainly true is that Joy has taken a product and made it better, then used her natural sales talent to bring it to a wide audience. It was pretty much inevitable that others would notice how good she was at marketing and ask for her help.

Chapter 8: Supporting Celebrities

Many celebrities lend their names to product lines. Sometimes it's a product they use themselves that's now being made available to the public; many athletes do this. Affordable versions of professional sports equipment often sell well, and usually it doesn't take much more than a celebrity endorsement to guarantee success. It can be more difficult when well-known personalities move outside their own field, though, as tennis star Serena Williams found out when she started planning her own line of fashion items. Williams was well known for her often quirky outfits both on and off court – she played the 2004 US Open in a denim skirt, for example – and has been building up a second career as a fashion designer for years. She's often said that while she had to work hard at developing her tennis skills design is something that comes naturally to her,[viii] but selling her creations is a different matter – especially when she came up with her Signature Statement collection. Based around jewelry and handbags, Williams set out to create a stylish but affordable line that was ideally suited to the shopping channel market.

The big question was: how to promote the products? Williams had the design skills, but what she didn't have was the knowledge of how to connect with an HSN audience and persuade them to pick up the phone. The solution was to form a partnership with someone who did have that knowledge, and there was an obvious choice: Joy Mangano. By 2009 Joy was by far the biggest seller on HSN, with a proven ability to turn almost any product she endorsed into a sales success. Williams realized that with Joy on board her products would have a huge head start on HSN. In April 2009 they formed a partnership to launch the range on HSN, with predictably impressive results.

The same year, New York model and lifestyle author Frank Sepe developed his own brand of health and fitness products, and decided to sell them through HSN. Again, he looked for an experienced partner to help launch his range, and again he picked Joy. They went on HSN together for the launch on July 28, and managed to sell out the entire stock in record time.

Other partnerships went beyond selling. When celebrity chef Todd English wanted to create a new range of pans, his first stop was Joy. English had some specific requirements: he wanted a professional-grade pan that anyone could use without complicated seasoning, which meant a non-stick finish, but he was concerned about the use of PTFE and other chemicals in the non-stick pans that were currently available. Joy's contacts, built up through her years of developing products, helped English come up with a new design that used a ceramic-based non-stick surface. GreenPan was first demonstrated on HSN by Joy and English in July 2007, and 24,000 pans were sold in just four hours.[ix]

Joy has helped to promote and market many other products on HSN, ranging from self-help books to Esteban guitars, but probably her highest-profile collaboration was with Iman, the model who's also known for being married to David Bowie. Iman made a name for herself on the catwalk from the late 1970s through to the mid-1990s, but shortly after her wedding to Bowie she began to scale back her modeling and took up a new range of activities. She devotes a lot of time to charity work, mainly aimed at protecting children, and finances her career with a range of products she designed. The first was a cosmetics line launched in 1994, inspired by her difficulty in finding makeup that suited her skin tone. Iman Cosmetics is still one of the top-selling brands of foundation, according to Walgreen's online sales figures, and brings in around $25 million a year.[x] Seeing that success, HSN chief executive Mindy Grossman decided that any beauty or fashion product designed or promoted by Iman would be a sure hit with shoppers, and approached the model to suggest it.

Iman, however, wasn't so convinced. "Clothing design should be left to the professionals," she said. Grossman wasn't about to give up so easily, though. Iman might not be a professional designer, but she wasn't a professional cosmetics creator either; her skill was in knowing instinctively what looked good. Grossman persuaded her to try an item she already liked – the kaftan. These lightweight, loose robes are widely worn throughout Asia and the Middle East, and while they're not common in Iman's native Somalia they are popular in Egypt, where she went to high school. She picked up a fondness for cashmere ones while she was at school and, ever since, had always owned several. At Grossman's urging she released her own line and sold them on HSN, where they proved popular.

Encouraged by the success of her kaftans, Iman decided to take Grossman's advice and develop more products; her plan was to create a line of handbags and small luggage. At this point she started talking to Joy. Iman knew what a good bag should look like; Joy, with her years of experience as an inventor, knew how to add practical features that worked and would attract buyers. Just as importantly, she had learned how to get a good design made to a high standard but at a reasonable price. Between them they developed a line of products that combined functionality and style at an affordable cost, including purses, totes and duffles. They presented the range together on HSN and, yet again, it turned into a winner – Iman's brand is now the number four top seller out of more than 200 fashion lines on HSN.

Style and practicality don't always go together. The classic example is high-heeled shoes. They've been a staple of women's (and often men's) fashion since at least the 9th century, but they're not exactly comfortable for most people and have also been linked with a range of health problems. It stands to reason that when many people prefer to wear sneakers to work and change into their "normal" shoes when they get there, or walk home from a party in their stockings with their shoes in their hands, there's probably something wrong with the shoes. That's exactly the sort of problem Joy enjoys solving, and in 2009 she started working with StrideRite – the makers of Keds – to come up with a range of shoes that would give the benefits of high heels in a more comfortable package. The result was Performance Platforms, which went on sale in 2010 – first as sneakers, then in a variety of other styles.

Chapter 9: Branching Out

Although Joy has achieved fame and fortune through designing and marketing products, she's never been afraid to try something different. It seems that the same talents that let her create new inventions and bring them to market can be used for other things too. Since the late 1990s she has branched out into entertainment and hospitality, and that's turned out pretty well too. Her first big non-sales achievement was the discovery of a guitarist.

Stephen Paul was the oldest of four children from a Pittsburgh, Pennsylvania family. Born in 1949, the son of a steelworker, the first time he ever saw a guitar was in a shop window when he was eight years old. An uncle bought it for him and, from that moment, he dedicated himself to learning how to play. When he started at Carnegie Mellon University in 1968 the school had just begun offering guitar as a subject, and Stephen selected that and English literature as joint majors. His guitar teacher was mediocre but that didn't dim Stephen's enthusiasm, and he managed to persuade Spanish master guitarist Andrés Segovia to take him on as a student after he graduated.[xi] From 1974 to 1978 he studied classical guitar at Segovia's studio in the northern Spanish city of Santiago de Compostela. When he returned to the USA he started touring, using the stage name Esteban – the Spanish version of his own name – and it looked like he was at the start of a successful career as a professional musician.

Unfortunately for Esteban, just a year after his first tour he was hit and badly injured by a drunk driver. The worst damage was to his left hand and arm, and it was more than a decade before he recovered enough to play the guitar again. The long enforced break had put a major dent in his career, though, and he had to start again at the beginning. In fact, at first, the only job he could get was playing as a house musician at the Hyatt Regency Hotel in Scottsdale, Arizona. As time passed he managed to start touring again, and released his first album in 1991, but it proved much harder to make the breakthrough than it had first time around. His revived career was moderately successful – a group of devoted fans started to crowd the Hyatt's bar five nights a week to see his performances - but he'd lost a lot of momentum after the accident. Then Joy saw him play.

Joy had built her career on her ability to see the potential in a new way of doing things. Now she saw the potential in Esteban as well. She was still with QVC at the time and invited Esteban to play on her show. Weeks later Barry Diller bought Ingenious Designs and Joy moved over to HSN. Because she'd signed Esteban up for a six-month exclusive contract with QVC she couldn't promote him again until the contract had expired, but as soon as she could she brought him on to HSN to play for her new audience. On June 29, 2000 he made the first of two appearances on the channel that summer, and sold a total of 132,000 CDs. Two of his albums made the Billboard Top 100. Esteban's career was suddenly, and dramatically, back in the fast lane.

Despite his renewed success, though, Esteban wasn't signed to a record company. Instead, Joy decided to do things her own way. Esteban sold CDs to Ingenious Designs; Joy, in turn, sold them to HSN. They each made a couple of dollars' profit on each disk – and that, for a musician, is a much better deal than they'd get in royalties from one of the traditional distributors. Today Esteban is still performing, still selling CDs and DVDs, and has started marketing his own line of guitars; it's all backed up by the selling power of HSN and Joy.

Helping promote Esteban's career was a big change from inventing and selling her own products, but her next step outside of the comfort zone was a much larger one. In 2009 she opened her own restaurant, Porto Vivo, in Huntington, together with Swiss restaurateur Philipp Seipelt. That's always a high-risk decision; a huge percentage of new restaurants don't survive their first couple of years because competition is stiff, and after the initial excitement it can be very hard to keep the tables busy. It isn't easy to strike the right balance. The vital zone between too unremarkable and too oddball isn't very wide, and many would-be restaurateurs don't manage to land in it.

True to form, Joy did. Attention to detail has always been a hallmark of her designs and she brought that same dedication to Porto Vivo. As the executive chef she picked Joseph Balbo, a fellow Long Island native from an Italian-American family who'd trained at the Italian Culinary Institute in Calabria.[xii] As you'd expect from Balbo's background and Joy's own Italian heritage, the restaurant's menu has a very strong Italian theme, with a modern touch. A great menu isn't enough to make a successful restaurant though; after all, the people who eat at upscale restaurants are often pretty good at cooking themselves. In order to thrive, a restaurant needs to deliver the whole package – surroundings and atmosphere as well as food and drinks. Joy made sure every aspect of Porto Vivo was as perfect as she could make it – the décor, the bar list, music, staff dress code. Tables are decorated with fresh bouquets, and menus are presented on iPads so diners can easily see images of what's on the menu. And it paid off. *Long Island Pulse* described Porto Vivo as "stylish and sophisticated". *Table With A View* listed it as one of the most exciting restaurants in Long Island and raved about the food.

Six years after it opened Porto Vivo remained as popular as ever and had firmly established itself as one of Huntington's most stylish places to eat. It's attracted favorable reviews from most of New York's leading restaurant critics. For a restaurateur affluent suburbs are at least as risky as city locations; a mediocre establishment might be able to survive in a small town where there's not much competition, but in a place like Huntington there isn't any shortage of alternatives if the experience isn't all that people want. Porto Vivo offers that experience, and that's a real testament to Joy's gift for giving people what they want.

Chapter 10: Living The Dream

With so many business ventures underway, it seems like Joy would have no time for any life outside of work. Amazingly, that's not the case. Her family is as close as ever. They've come a long way from the cramped ranch house they were living in when she invented the Miracle Mop, though. Now Joy owns a 42,000 square foot French-style mansion that sits on a landscaped ten-acre North Shore plot. She's had it extensively remodeled since she bought it and now its features include a huge indoor pool linked to the main house by a covered walkway, and a tennis court sits in the grounds. Inside there are 14 bedrooms and 13 bathrooms.

In traditional Italian style Joy sees her company as very much a family business. Her ex-husband, Tony Miranne, is executive vice president of sales. They've been divorced for more than twenty years but are still on friendly terms, and Tony is in awe of Joy's business skills; "Joy truly possesses the inner drive to achieve what she wants to achieve", he says.[xiii] Meanwhile, the vice president of brand product development and strategic marketing is another family member – her oldest daughter Christie. After graduating from Providence College Christie started in the Ingenious Designs office and quickly worked her way up. She's young to be so senior in a major corporation, but perhaps she's inherited her mother's drive and determination.

It looks like Joy's other daughters have their fair share of her talent, too. Although neither of the younger two has followed her into the business, they're both looking quite successful in their own right. Bobby studied law at Columbia and now works for one of New York's top legal firms. The youngest, Jackie, is a graduate of State University of New York's Fashion Institute of Technology, and after that signed up with leading model agency Major International. She has also appeared as a model in the Bravo Network show *Project Runway* and has been featured in several leading fashion magazines, including *Cosmopolitan*.

Bobby and Jackie might follow their older sister into Joy's business one day – or all three might set up their own companies. As Joy herself says, they've all experienced the excitement of creating a large business from nothing.[xiv] They all played their own parts in the rise of Ingenious Designs from struggling startup to its current status; without their help, in the early days, Joy's workload might have been just too much for even her to handle. Now, they know that if you have some talent and determination it's possible to achieve just about anything you want. Too many young people have business ideas but are deterred from pursuing them by well-meaning parents who'd rather see them in a secure job with a guaranteed salary; there's not much chance of that happening to Joy's daughters. If any of them decides to be an entrepreneur they'll have the confidence to go for it and the full backing of their mother. The youngest looks like she's already taking the first steps to building her own brand through her website, JackieAtHome.com.

Joy herself doesn't show any signs of slowing down. Now in her late fifties she's still as busy as ever promoting her products and working on ideas for new ones. For someone like her this is a very exciting time. Despite the recent economic crisis demand for consumer products is still high, perhaps higher than ever. At the same time people are looking for good value and that's what Joy's products provide. She has always aimed to give her customers innovative designs at an affordable price, and right now that's exactly what consumers want. In fact, among home shopping fans her name is now synonymous with distinctive, sometimes even quirky, items that manage to make life easier by eliminating little hassles. She doesn't work in high-tech areas; we're not likely to see a Joy Mangano smartphone or tablet computer any time soon. Consumer electronics aren't everything, though, and one of the ironies of modern society is that while we use devices – tablets, GPS, the internet, TVs and many more – that would have been the stuff of science fiction when the Miracle Mop went on sale, a lot of the other things we use every day follow basic designs that haven't changed in decades or even centuries. Often we struggle with simple problems simply because nobody's ever bothered to think of a solution. Christie remembers, on a holiday to the Hamptons, watching a man come out of a bakery with two pies in his hands and struggle to unlock his car. Joy was watching, too, and a year later she showcased her new bakery box design on HSN.[xv] According to her daughters, that's how she uses the time other women with her wealth would spend by the pool – by thinking up solutions to the problems she's seen.

Of course, technology is likely to make it a lot easier for Joy in the future. When she was developing the Miracle Mop the design and prototyping process was a slow, painful one. All her concept drawings were done by hand, and the actual blueprints drawn up by the engineer she worked with. To make a prototype meant creating molds for each of the plastic components, an expensive process when you just plan to make a few test samples. Every time a component needed to be altered that meant a new mold, and more expense. Now it's easy to create designs on a computer and view them on screen exactly as they'll look in real life. Digital designs can be sent straight to a 3D printer and turned into prototypes within hours. 3D printing is still a slow and expensive process but it's much cheaper than the traditional way. Molds only need to be made once the design is finalized and ready to go into production, so now Joy can develop new products more efficiently than ever.

As far as her personal life goes, she's still single. She's on friendly terms with her ex-husband, but beyond that doesn't have time to date. "Who would marry someone who works seven days a week, 24 hours a day?" she asks.[xvi] That's a slight exaggeration but not very much of one; just running Ingenious Designs is a heavy workload, and on top of that she's still inventing and still appearing on HSN at least a couple of hours every week. It just takes a quick look at HSN to see that her products still play a major role in the network's business; there are new versions of My Little Steamer, a smart beach bag with built-in cooler, a new line of deluxe leather baggage, slippers that keep your feet warm in winter and different slippers that keep your feet cool in summer. There's a whole range of closet-organizing products, bedding, beauty cases and, of course, a massive selection of Huggable Hanger sets – still HSN's best-selling product ever.

Conclusion

Joy Mangano's story is an amazing one. A smart child and gifted teenager, it was always clear she had the potential to succeed – but to this extent? When she appears on HSN in person she generates average sales of more than $1 million per hour; the products she's personally invented bring the network more than $150 million every year. She holds more than a hundred patents on products or features she's designed herself and is rated as one of the most creative 100 business people in the world.[xvii] What's the secret?

If you ask Joy, she'd probably say the secret is hard work. It usually is, in business as in anything else, although hard work on its own is rarely enough. Successful people normally have some latent talent that effort will make the most of, and that's definitely the case with Joy. She has a mind that naturally understands technical problems and can come up with new ways of solving them; she looks at the ways we *could* make things instead of just how we *do* make them. It's impossible to succeed as an inventor if you don't put in the hard work to refine your ideas, get them into production and promote them to potential buyers – but it's also impossible to succeed if you don't have the ideas in the first place.

Most of us do come up with good ideas, though; the problem is that, usually, we never do anything with them. That's the lesson Joy learned at age 16, when she thought of a fluorescent flea collar – only to see a big corporation release an almost identical product months later. Deep down we're all potential inventors so I'll leave the last word to Joy Mangano herself:

"If it's anywhere near a realistic goal, I say, 'Go for it' because, look at me!"

[i] Investors.com (Jul 19, 2010); *Joy Mangano Cleans Up In Sales*
http://news.investors.com/management-leaders-and-success/071910-540758-joy-mangano-cleans-up-in-sales-.htm
[ii] ABC News (Mar 31, 2006); *Making Millions Off a Super Mop*
http://abcnews.go.com/print?id=1782048
[iii] New York Times (Feb 11, 2001); *Cleaning Up in Business, With a Mop*
http://www.nytimes.com/2001/02/11/nyregion/cleaning-up-in-business-with-a-mop.html
[iv] St. Petersburg Times (Jul 30, 2002); *It all started with 112 can openers*

http://www.sptimes.com/2002/07/30/Floridian/It_started_with_112_c.shtml
[v] New York Times (Feb 11, 2001); *Cleaning Up in Business, With a Mop*
http://www.nytimes.com/2001/02/11/nyregion/cleaning-up-in-business-with-a-mop.html
[vi] Ernst & Young; *EY Entrepreneur of the Year Hall of Fame*
http://www.ey.com/US/en/About-us/Entrepreneurship/Entrepreneur-Of-The-Year/US_EOY_Article_EOY_HOF
[vii] RolyKit BV; *Company history*
http://rolykit.nl/Company/company.html
[viii] Fox News (Nov 14, 2004); *Serena Williams Keen on Fashion Career*
http://www.foxnews.com/story/2004/11/14/serena-williams-keen-on-fashion-career.html
[ix] PR Newswire (Aug 6, 2007); *Environmentally-Friendly GreenPan(TM) Cookware Sells Out in Four Hours*
http://www.prnewswire.com/news-releases/environmentally-friendly-greenpantm-cookware-sells-out-in-four-hours-during-

the-world-launch-exclusively-on-hsn-57892517.html
[x] New York Times (Jun 4, 2010); *Iman: Not Just Another Pretty Face*
https://web.archive.org/web/20100607092303/http://www.ny times.com/2010/06/06/fashion/06IMAN.html
[xi] Esteban Music; *Biography*
http://estebanmusic.com/esteban-biography/
[xii] Porto Vivo; *About Us*
http://www.porto-vivo.com/about.html
[xiii] ABC News (Mar 31, 2006); *Making Millions Off a Super Mop*
http://abcnews.go.com/print?id=1782048
[xiv] New York Times (Feb 11, 2001); *Cleaning Up in Business, With a Mop*
http://www.nytimes.com/2001/02/11/nyregion/cleaning-up-in-business-with-a-mop.html
[xv] ABC News (Mar 31, 2006); *Making Millions Off a Super Mop*
http://abcnews.go.com/print?id=1782048
[xvi] Newsday (Sep 10, 2014); *Entertainment*
http://www.newsday.com/entertainment...ostemailedlink
[xvii] Investors.com (Jul 19, 2010); *Joy Mangano Cleans Up In Sales*
http://news.investors.com/management-leaders-and-success/071910-540758-joy-mangano-cleans-up-in-sales-.htm